Advance praise for *Sharp Blue Search of Flame*

"*Sharp Blue Search of Flame* is a collection of poems that reminds us, with every syllable and every line, that both the spiritual and, dare I say, the carnal can reside together sublimely. In a world in which we have to ask, daily, 'What do you want? To be God, man, or beast?' Zilka Joseph teaches us that we find each inside every one of us, and they all hold some beauty, particularly in her masterful hands. She asks, 'Can our whirring hearts hold steady?' But how can we, faced with so much truth along this journey?"
—A. Van Jordan

"Zilka Joseph writes vivid, sensuous, eloquent poems from a world of dual cultures—India where she was born, and America where she now makes her home. Hindi festivals, epic heroes, the natural surroundings of Garuda, King of Birds, and cosmic mythology mix in with airports, skycaps, Bob Dylan on 45s, immigrant loneliness, and a classic Christian night prayer. Her's is a delicate eye tracing fish, birds, and flowers, yet a sense of adventure prevails in her long lines as they leap across the page, giving us a sense of fearlessness that makes Joseph an especially enticing poet. I look forward to reading more of her zestful work."
—Colette Inez, author of *The Luba Poems*

"A cause for rejoicing among true lovers of poetry, *Sharp Blue Search of Flame* is a rich gathering by a genuinely gifted poet, blessed with a voice that is all at once ancient and modern and redolent with fabulous surprises."
—Lorna Goodison, poet

"Rich with the scents and sounds and colors of her native Kolkota, Zilka Joseph's poetry is also haunted: by the real and imagined violence of the world, by the losses entailed in migration, by the loved ones left behind. Deeply felt and lushly rendered, these poems weave a tapestry of sorrow and celebration, tenderness and outrage, bodily longing and bodily vulnerability. A book as searching as its title. And in flame."
—Linda Gregerson

SHARP BLUE
SEARCH OF FLAME

Made in Michigan Writers Series

General Editors

Michael Delp, Interlochen Center for the Arts

M. L. Liebler, Wayne State University

Advisory Editors

Melba Joyce Boyd, *Wayne State University*

Stuart Dybek, *Western Michigan University*

Kathleen Glynn

Jerry Herron, *Wayne State University*

Laura Kasischke, *University of Michigan*

Thomas Lynch

Frank Rashid, *Marygrove College*

Doug Stanton

Keith Taylor, *University of Michigan*

A complete listing of the books in this series can be found online at wsupress.wayne.edu

SHARP BLUE

SEARCH OF FLAME

poems by Zilka Joseph

Wayne State University Press
Detroit

Manufactured in the United States of America.

20 19 18 17 16   5 4 3 2 1

ISBN 978-0-8143-4049-3 (paperback)
ISBN 978-0-8143-4050-9 (e-book)

Library of Congress Control Number: 2015948596

Publication of this book was made possible
by a generous gift from The Meijer Foundation.
Additional support was provided by Michigan
Council for Arts and Cultural Affairs and
National Endowment for the Arts.

Goddess image on p. 34 © istockphoto.com/
AjayShrivastava
Tiger image on p. 56 © istockphoto.com/Oksanita

Designed and typeset by Bryce Schimanski
Composed in Adobe Caslon Pro

*This book is for my mother, Ruby Joseph (née Benjamin),
and for my father, Solomon (Sunny) Aaron Joseph,
who passed in 2012 and 2014 respectively.*

*And always for John, who tenderly cared for my parents
and mourns their loss with me.*

CONTENTS

Apples and Oranges

There never were any apples in Eden.
Only oranges—vibrant suns shining,

fruit of dust and heat that warmed to her pulse
beating stronger and brighter,

fruit of earth itself. She was ripe like the sun
before she even thirsted, reached and opened

her petals to the radiance fragrant in her palm,
before the lush fire licked her tongue

and before the coiled serpent of Creation
threw her into subterranean shadow.

She knew she would always be the sun
even when the gates closed behind her

and though History would try new tricks,
twist orange to apple,

the men with missing bones,
the snakes, would stay the same.

Consider the Sari,

all nine long yards of it, or even six,
           and cherish every inch. Understand

the language of the loom,
           hands, art, the blood and body

of cotton, of silk,
           the secret of draping its serpentine grace

so you can look like a goddess.
           They wound it around us,

let it wrap us in its womb,
           its mother-love of woven fabric. We laughed

as we tripped on the petticoat's web,
           got caught in tassel traps, saw how

it teased, seduced, learned to tame it. The pallavs
           flowed over our shoulders, the cloth

sweeping around and behind us
           like a river dyed the color of peacocks,

or spring rice, or godhuli—shades of dusk
           and dust when the cows came home. Imagining

we were starlets, or queens
           in boardrooms, courts, and parliament,

we grew vain. But forbidden to think
           beyond the walls

built by the patriarchs, we inherit
           the destiny

of our mothers, and Draupadi's
           sorrow. The folds fall heavy

around our ankles. Smoothing pleats,
            we hide our navels, cover

midriffs. The red marriage sari
            has zari embroidery, sindur fills

the parting of our hair, and when
            our husbands come to us at night

they throw the gold-red swirls over our heads,
            our cries muffled in its unraveling

thread. Pallavs must hang low
            for no one should see our faces,

and we fear to look beyond its fringe,
            the border's hemmed edge,

for we are flesh of the air
            wrapped in woven shells,

live briefly. Like silkworms
            inside cocoons

dropped in boiling water,
            we give our lives

to ageless hands
            who weave patterns

dreamed by the fathers,
            and dress our sweet brides,

swathe our sisters,
            swaddle our girl-children,

shroud our own silent bones
            in its weft of darkness.

Something Falls

Something falls
silent

the night we return
from the chariot festival

to celebrate Lord Jagannath;
the last time I'll come home

with the face of a flushed and happy
six-year-old just back from a street fair,

the smell of cigarette smoke and sweaty crowds
pressed on my flesh like perfume

when pushing my way
like a mole through soil

for a seat on the small wooden Ferris wheel—
tumbling-boxes we called them,

painted a lurid red and yellow, tilting dangerously,
overloaded, and moaning like an animal

in pain. It is late when we walk home,
a long way. Running to keep up with my neighbors

and a friend of my father's who
has never witnessed this lavish Hindu festival,

 a sailor called Salvador from Bombay
and whose ship is in town. I am in love

with him, all three and a half feet of me—
in love with his name, his beaked nose,

his stories of dogs, the sea, Jesus. How I blush
when he visits. Everyone teases me

as he blows me a kiss when he leaves. I never
sleep that night. Neither do my father,

mother, or grandmother. Holding me
in turn, they knead my aching thighs and calves,

as wave after wave breaks within me, my muscles
convulsing. My father curses the neighbors

 who made a child of six walk such a distance,
my mother's high voice says, *she has fever,*

wipes my sweat, lays her soft lips on my forehead;
granny mutters, *girls shouldn't be*

roaming around like this anyway . . . ; and I
writhe on the bed,

suck in their terror like a black hole

while some wrathful angel

leaps off nightmare's ladder
to wrestle my flailing limbs to the ground,

and watches as I drag my wounded body

the way I will do
for the rest of my life.

The Blessed

wings still glossy, she's slouched

in the shade of the marauding fig
wild roots swallowing
cracked bricks

at the lip of our kitchen window
she waits, lopsided

tail ragged
as if rat-bitten

gaze deeper than hunger

my hands scrape down my plate
some meat I leave on the bones
extra grains of rice

she hops near
balancing this edge

who will care for us, little sister
we who are broken but not by our own hands

tap-tapping her beak
she picks cleanly

it's for bullies I keep watch
my eyes scour the sun-white rectangle of sky

small cousin of the rook
and of the hard-beaked raven
how cruel are our kind

do we not bleed do we not die
we are not ravaged by fury but fear

so eat at my house, my one-eyed beauty
rest here then O bent-bodied bird

my wild, starved, one-legged one

Where Sparrows Nest

above ceiling fans
and in the cement ventilators mynahs

sing and screech all afternoon
like children practicing

scales, here within these sun-filled
walls, my parents live. This red

brick building was young once,
banyan saplings now thrive in its cracks,

and inside, large rooms and high ceilings
offer spiders a home. The mice

find ways into the three refrigerator-
turned-cupboards and the oven

stuffed with plastic bags and string. Bulbuls,
sometimes a golden oriole, still visit

the small medley of trees in the afternoon.
Crows are the kings

of the breezy verandah, conquering
more territory every day, hiding

their bloody treasures even under cushions,
behind old books, the photo

of Robert Redford, the tiger cub
poster in my room. My parents keep

those doors closed. They are Adam and Eve,
aged now, amid a forest

they can't let go. A ragged Eden
I never left. Where teak

furniture made long ago to order
is strong, though the upholstery

wore away and cotton
sheets cover it now. It gets a fresh

skin of soot every day. The walls
have grown darker, but it's always bright

in the late-day sun. Frailer
than the dust motes, my parents.

I am already thinking of my next flight,
over the Atlantic, the Caspian Sea,

the Arabian desert, the Hindu Kush
Mountains, the holy Ganga,

the rush up two flights of stairs,
mumble a quick Shema—

will I see their faces? Feel their thin
arms, sweet embraces? Or find

empty shells, a handful
of dusty feathers?

You, Without Shoes

we imagine you with a pen between your teeth
in an electric city

how you escaped the mud
its fierce love of flesh and bone

child, barefoot in the mud you walked
savored the squelching
deep now

the suck of soil around your ankles
your feet have sunk

how do you know

how to lift up
escape the pull of it

our child
gone away

you once were lustrous with rain
your feet like petals

trail of paisley print behind you
we grasped it in our hands
we could not let go

each foot searches
like a prayer before

it takes your weight

shoeless you played
how could we imagine you

all grown up
you, a woman with dreams held like a rose in her teeth

who never let the heels of our history
wear her down

we are old, we have not moved, we stay the same
we cannot understand
distance

we, the ones left behind
who fall

earth calls us daily

but you
you just shake us from your hair

shake the water from your feet
mud invisible

lift off
never look back

Penelope Speaks to the Women

And what it is about the Siren's song
that alarms us time and time again? Here,
even at home, calls up some dark panic
from the cave of our bellies, the hollows
of our woman-bones? A feathered terror
flies into our throats. Airborne music claws
and tears the smooth arc of our sea and sky;
And why is it we hope our men resist
that song, abroad, or here in Ithaca?
We know men sail a different sea than ours.
At night our sleep is restless. Hands tremble
as we weave and thread, do our daily chores.
When mighty gods have fallen to that song—
what then of lesser mortals of this world?

Prey

I heard about your grand catch,
bridegroom with tux and mansion,
jewelry, roses, and all.

Heard he beat your face in.
Tore you up like paper
white as the sheets

of your nuptial bed.
Flung you, many a night, still
kicking, into the snow.

Neighbors drew pretty
curtains against your cries. Some
sheltered you, but then

you went back to wear more purple
badges than your creamy skin
could hold. He left you,

so you found another. And
another. They stubbed your own
Kool Lights on you till

you were a pillar
of ash. And you search,
and you lure, trap them

with your sewn-up
painted mouth
when you stalk in wild places.

Seeking the Snake

What I find
when I look for you

is the wispy accordion of skin
you shed among the stones.

Sometimes
it has your face

imprinted in the filigree
of pale eyes and lips.

I read
the shape

of still-soft scales,
the texture roughening

even as I touch,
and just when I think

I've learned
a little more about you,

found something of myself
in the dusty diamonds

of your sloughed past—
it crumples,

gray ashes
cobwebbing

my palms.

Dharamsala

Who were you when I slept tucked against your body,
who was I when I woke with the sun in my eyes

blinded by the promise of day so exquisite

that it undid my blouse
and our songs drowned the colors of heaven;

passion caught us by the throat
like the scarf of purple silk you bought me
in a shop in the crowded cobbled streets of Dharamsala,

store keeper smiling. Wood smoke
from pavement tea shops
curled around Buddhist pilgrims and tourists
and maroon-robed figures spilling from buses,
pointing at posters of Richard Gere,

of the Dalai Lama beaming compassion upon the world,

his followers and locals filling the towns,
razing daily the virgin mountains of Himachal
to build hotels, houses for the holy,

for seekers,

for the wretched and the rich,
for loud tourists and shy honeymooners.
And there we were

trekking to Bhagsunath
which I remembered, one overcast winter day in my early youth
I had watched its carved lion heads black with age

spout ice-green water from grotesque jaws
into the temple bath
where devotees dipped their barely clad bodies

and gained blessing, maybe salvation.
Those who climb the steep path to visit it

they say are blessed;

we tried to keep that expectation alive
but stopped halfway,
exhausted. I sat by a hovel,
on a stone that covered a drain,

women draped in shawls walking effortlessly by.
One stopped, seeing me wilt near her wall,
offered tea and said,

you must reach Bhagsunath.

We sipped masala chai,
probed each others' faces
with hungry eyes
and you said,

why are we doing this?
Half-laughing, half-fainting in the heat
I don't know, I said.
Helping me to my feet
we stumbled down like happy drunks,
found a taxi, fell

into each others' arms
as it grunted up the bumpy slope
toward Judge Mahajan's bungalow—
grand as the Raj,

and next to it our rented cottage
crouched like a wild mushroom at the feet
of the Dhauladhar range. Wrapped

in blankets of rough spun wool,
Himalayan winds and Mozart's horn concertos

thumping the panes, we fell into sleep

as gently as the snowfall we watched cover
peaks above us shining salmon and gold with sunset.
Next morning, clasped

in the palms of a sunless sky,
we saw thunderstorms ravage trees,

and lightning throw thorns across the floor.

Like Blood

was shed
        by the bronze lamp in the corner,
                right by the lip of the dog-eared dictionary
                        near the open Scrabble board—

the letters anxious for someone's move,
        and the couch, just out of reach, where
                someone tried to stop them falling but couldn't,
                        and when the fall came, it was brief,

almost beautiful. Petals looking
        like a red dragon sketched on handmade paper,
                its tail a plume of fire and so like
                        the one they saw when they visited Sikkim,

the dragon dancers beneath the blazing silk
        drunk on chhaang as they
                ploughed through people and children,
                        excited strays nipping their heels,

and later, only scarlet shreds littered the crooked streets.
        Like Japanese koi suspended in marble ponds,
                mouthing the surface crimson,
                    open as roses

waiting—
some hide, throbbing in
        shadows of pale water lilies,
                and rippled where they fell
                        as she threw the buds—

the dyed beauties,
        so hopeful, and curled
                like fetuses, petals
                        clotting purple on the jute carpet.

Night Watchmen

On the landing

                    shifty angels huddle

lovers of cocaine

these half wraiths hunched
outside our Kolkata apartment

                    on the landing dark

as a young girl I chanted

when I lurched up the never-ending steps
and before I slept and when I visit now

                    Now I lay me down to sleep

they never raise their heads
or look us in the eye

near the walls in smoky air they melt
when I ring the bell

                    I hold my breath till

mum or dad slowed by age
will open the door

to sleep to sleep

                    how I prayed then with folded hands

the prayer
my grandma learned in school

breathe in breathe out
the men shield a flaring match, hold their breath

                    Now I lay me down to sleep

when the stairs are bright with evening sun
thick vapor fogs the panes

                 breathe in breathe out

stifling heat
their candles cast pale waves

                 I pray I pray thee Lord

this slender teak door is a veil
pulled over our small lives our eyes

our trembling in the shadow of our door posts
our trembling like the fingers of these men

starless night *Thy love*
the match flickers and dies

                 I pray thee Lord thy child to keep

the light the hallway light we turn off at night
the light replaced a hundred times

                 O keep dear Lord keep

our mezuzah stolen
the lamp ripped out every night

the broken bulb
swinging on its bare red wire

                 we bar the door
                 and prepare to sleep

but the men with slanted faces
never go never go

                 Thy love go with

these men who have blackened the walls
with sooty fingers *Thy love thy love*
made murals of spit and handprints

these shadows of men
hold handfuls of blue flames

Thy love go with me all the night

foil-crackle and white dust
whispers echo in the throat of the stairs
Wake me Lord Wake me

some men fall at sunrise as if dead
some half-waking stir *Thy love*
some do not wake do not

Wake me O Lord,
with the morning light

and the eyes who watch our helpless door
never sleep never sleep never sleep

Harbingers

Who calls? Who wakes? Saw
whet? Screech or horned
owl? October leaves shaken

from sleeping branches,
shuddering as they fell? I heard a rustle
and shove on the wind, a small cry

lifted on silent wings. But last night I awoke
remembering the jackals I heard
in the hills of south India. It was winter, my breath

made little clouds. The howling pack
slunk closer. From the windows
of that century-old bungalow I saw them spill

from the shrubs heavy with bloodred
coffee berries into the dim halo
of the garden light. They wandered

near the banks of fern, then faded, wailing
from a distance. In Michigan, the stricken
crows that fell daily like rain

have risen again. Their restless
cacophony shakes the trees this morning.
One nesting female stares

from the flaming sumac. She's just like our raucous
regular back home in Kolkata who haunted
our kitchen window for years, then disappeared—

childhood friend with the twisted
beak, gobbling the scraps we threw her
after Rabiya gutted the chicken. I hear frantic

caws, and Rabiya says, *Yah Allah! Sunoh baba!*
Listen child, she's telling you something.

Kingdom of Sharks

You think they swim far away
 in the deep, deep oceans

where you say

you never go. But what about the sharks whose

fins never break the surface of your well-lit home aquarium—
complete with a plastic diver in a wet suit

exploring remains

of ships,
ancient pagodas,
a lost Atlantis;

and those who hide,

watch you circle inside your bubble,

dash from shadows to eat your money,
your clothes,

and the ones whose bodies talk to you—

take your woman, or man,
maybe make your house disappear. And the ones that

ram you like runaway eighteen-wheelers with three rows of teeth.

You guessed it, these aren't tidy feeders,

and no, they don't
swallow you whole—

just drown you in the wine of your own blood,

break your body bit by bit like bread.

Then, think about

the mighty angels of death—
those who do not pass over though
your door posts bear the sign,

but stop to visit;

and those who stay to flay your flesh,
shackle your ankles,

force you to serve them forever. And when they move on,

they make way for others more terrible. The kind

obsessed with detail—

who will wipe out

even the last wisp
of your skin, a shred of fingernail

that happened to escape;

the ones who destroy
every relic,

leave no evidence

of their existence or yours.

Bird in a Blizzard

this is when you know
you should have stayed home

this is when you know this is
not your element

when you know
you have been blown way off course

that water changes its face every day
and the faces you love blur
in that churning

that the whispers in the thick flood of flakes

come from elsewhere
that the ones who gave you shelter

are gone

that the cracking of the spine
of the frozen river
will be the last sound you will hear

the *thump thump thump*
you hear in your head
is someone trapped inside your heart

yes this is when you know
your ancestors are wanderers
singing tunes you never knew you knew

you remember
every word of the song
that the wind rips apart and flings

but how quickly your throat fills with snow

and when you turn again   you shiver as if you are wingless

you can move
in only one direction now

          deeper

The Eye of the Poppy

knows where the valley of shadow lies.
It is the valley
of mothers searching
for their children.

Here, red petals stream
in the wind and catch
in the hair of the women
who wander this place
of silence. Look, here they come,
the mothers searching
for their children. Shh! Do not
startle them. They walk slowly
beside the still waters,
gather red petals, hold them
in their palms. These are the last
gifts from their children.
Children who crave
the touch of a vanished
hand. Red spills like wine
through their fingers. They leave
behind them a trail of petals
that the children will find.
The mothers have not slept
since they were lifted
from their bodies, have walked
for miles in the night,
been afraid but their bloodstained feet
never stop moving. Nor their torn
hands. Do not disturb
these mothers! Their eyes are
lanterns lighting their way

through fields of darkness.

break break break   the gray day is just begun

the sun   is broken
in the valley of shattered hearts
there is only shadow

no table laid out   for grieving mothers
soft are the fragments
of poppies and silken
are their strewn bodies.

petals land on the still waters   sail like little boats

rest like ruby drops of holy oil   upon the head of every mother
when she walks through   her shadow
                              into endless shadow
and where
is the shepherd the staff the psalm
only petal rain   gray shadow upon shadow

Here, where the petals flow like red rivers, my mother roams
She who was surprised by sudden darkness, sudden pain of light
She whose last breath flew up like a dove

I remember her eyes
There are petals that were her eyes, her dance eyes

The poppy I hold closes its eye
and will not show me the way
I will rip apart
these red veils these silken lies

O my mother. Gone from my sight forever.
She slipped too quickly through the black-lashed eye of the poppy.

Who killed her? "I," said cock robin. "With my bow and arrow."
"I," said the fly. "I saw her die. With my little eye. I saw her die."

The sand and bone wilderness has consumed her.
The heat shimmers up from the dunes.
Still she searches. Look, here she comes.
She holds the petals I scattered over her fallen
body, her frail bamboo bier. *Who saw her die?*
Was there any peace for her in that wretched hall
filled with so many dead and so many mourning?
Could she see the black billows of smoke,
the hissing furnaces? We paid the men
what they wanted. We could not bargain
for her bones. We brought home
ashes. Our throats were filled
with thorns. Wilderness of sand and bone.
Ashes in a clay jar meant for water.

After the flames,
did she cross the river? Who rowed her? Took her hand then?
Where the shepherd? Psalmist? Psalm? Where
the piper at the gates of dawn?

O for *the touch of a vanished hand*
picking petals like pearls from the sea,
her voice singing high and sweet,
her cotton robe red with flaring poppies and cabbage-green leaves
as she wraps her arms around me and sings
you are my sunshine

Sunshine. It is a hot humid afternoon. Was I just four?
A sunbeam streams through the window. It is a bridge
of light and fine dust touching us both.

I try to catch the dust motes. Then I turn,
open my palms to show her, but the room spins.

Her hair is silver fire and her skin
is the rippled sea and the wind begins to howl.

the gray day has just begun

the vanished
I will say Kaddish for you for a hundred years, mother.
Yes, I a woman—and yes, alone.
What minyan can stop me?
What God, man, or beast?

O cruel psalmist, do not disturb her!
It was you who stole
her voice from me. You
who tore her into a thousand
petals and scattered her flesh
across the dunes. Sing all you want,
deceitful psalmist! I have ears only for her song.

the red petals *break break break*
how hard the waves smash upon our separate shores

I will reach her

in spite of the valley
which opens

                              like a black-lashed eye
she will find me

                              in spite of your veils
                              your vale of faces your honeyed lies
                              your song your lyre your seductive eyes
we will meet

                              where petals
                              become whole again

❀

Move on, singer with lips like wine,
promises like heady poppies

full of dew. Look behind you.
The mothers have learned

your secret. They are not afraid

of your vales of nothingness. Your shallow promises. Your shadow
heaven. Your paper hell. Your hollow lions
and cotton-wool lambs. Your mighty
deserts and sandstorms. They will
walk through your thorns
and find us. Look,

her hands are petals of fire! Flowers
I scattered over her
like tears.

She walks toward me now
singing
you are my sunshine, my only sunshine

I see the lamps that are her eyes

Havan

—*Sacrifice;* sacrificial fire used for Hindu ceremonies

he got angrier they lifted
    the blue plastic can
        from the kitchen
            floor my hand
                haldi-streaked
                    I cried out I backed
                        away ran toward
                            the bedroom the old lady
                                  held onto my sari pallav
                                            pulled
                            me hard she was seventy
                      but she was strong I could
                see her betel-stained
            teeth close to my face
        jagged yellow bone
      cage door opening
    fingers like steel hinges
  creaking Krishna Krishna
pay my dowry

O Krishna

I have no children
    murmuring in the pipal trees
        rain of thin glass
            bangles breaking
                mouth full flood
                    of kerosene
                        generous as love
                            blue god flesh
                                on fire like sindur
                                    in my hair easily, caught
                            like ghee and grain
                    eaten whole
                take it all take
            O witness
          union divine
        no holy Ganga water
      no sweetness
    like jasmine
or sandalwood this

burning   this flame   eternal

Fire: For Beginners

                Breathe in deep and blow
softly as if drying wet clay,
and spell it out,

say *faaah*—like a

long cry of pain;

              then say *i*
(pronounced *eye*),
pushed with force—

like Adam and Eve
by a scarlet sirocco,

expelled
by the seraph
hot with holy rage;

              next say *ire*,
let your tongue lash
the virgin
syllable of

anger—
              orphan of fear
and heartbreak searching for
a name. What lesson

this? Divine

disillusion? Light gone
wrong? What being
could not contain

the raging
                conflagration? In wrath,
desire, dreams, and ash live
the alpha and omega

of flame. Burnt child, see these scars!
We are all branded young.

The Bharatnatyam Dancer

Imagine this: It's Shiva's Rudra tandava
my mother performs

frenzied
dance of destruction

her lotus feet

scorching
the earth with flame

not the great god's three wild locks
or river Ganga
bursting through matted curls

       but her thick black rope of hair
       whipping

the backs
of her knees. Her sari pleats
open and close

the pallav's silken sweep bound
in a belt of gold

How thunderous

her kohled eyes, how pure
the gestures of her ever-changing
mudras. But where was

your   fury   O sweet mother

Nataraj, where your protective flame?

Did your three eyes
freeze unweeping

and deaf your holy ears

to her
to the sounds of a hundred brass
ghungurus

thrumming on her ankles

No No   you heard her feet the bells the beat of lighting feet
you heard

her desire you heard
her steps her dance shatter Mount Kailash
your home your god-abode your manly
kingdom
you heard the audience
roar

and knew all along   her father's will
that he would say to her
No more!   The tongue

the tongue of every ankle bell

ripped out   her heart a tomb
her art her fame
turned to cinders by you

you jealous, jealous lord of dance

Mudras: Language of Hands

—written to accompany a triptych of photographs depicting
  hand gestures of classical Indian dance

I.

Speak then to me

what tales
these fingers tell

the waking, the calling
the eye

body

words
carved in air

between the lines

of the hands

                              of the hands

                       between the lines
                          carved in air

                                words
                                body

                              the eye
                 the waking, the calling

                       these fingers tell
                            what tales

                       speak then to me

40

2.

Clap of wing, deer call

              do you hear butterflies

fingertip-language
on cave walls awake

             what roams

moonless

a buffalo turns his head
the breathing jungle

feelers aquiver
they wait

             listen

heartbeat of cricket-song

             shell of silence

my palms press back
the darkness

see this lamp I make
             how deep its bowl

the longing soul
how tall its tongue

its sharp blue   search of flame

3.

O my mouth

has many tongues
                        myriad voices

swift
the blood in my veins

                    like hawks
                            my wrists dive

and soar
making love to the night
my arms become

                        ten snakes

my three eyes
of lightning
                        strike the earth

the drummer drums
                        in my skin
                                the dance begins

again

Turntable

When Dad brought the silver-gray
Garrard home, I rushed to see,

breathe the holy, plastic-oil smell,
feel the shiny steel, the springy

record bed. I was six.
Beatles it was, from morning till night,

the big green apple spinning madly,
the 45s stacked atop the magic

tower, turning into a swirling black
pool, ring within ring

within ring racing around. My breath
steamed up my pink framed

glasses, I watched the stylus lift off,
glide, and perch

like a stiff bird on the inner
edge of the record and sink

automatically onto the whirling dervish
of a disc. "Money can't buy me love,"

"It's been a hard day's night,"
"I saw her standing there," I sang

while I wrote pages in cursive
for mean Mrs. Rice, sang at the table,

sang in my sleep. I danced with my teenaged sister
and brother every night. Our ankles

were slender, my moves so fast
when I jived. Steps my feet remembered

after they brought me back
from hospital. Dad carrying me up the stairs,

my limbs like dead wood.

The Hands That Lit the Shabbat Lamps

My mother's hands—what did they dream?

Tough and weathered they are,
heavy, thick, square-
                nailed, strong; did a lifetime

of labor

in a man's world; bore the weight of all our needs,
the brunt

of a mother-in-law's tongue, Dad's quick temper. How hard
those pale hands slaved—

tinted with turmeric, smelling of garlic, cilantro,
or cloves, cinnamon and butter on high holidays
and at night Pond's Cold Cream. For special

times she wore
nail polish for silk sari evenings, or gold jewelry events
Dad's official dinners, for weddings. The rougher

her fingers grew, the more

she slid into her shell,
hiding her true heart. Just as her mother's

had even before the fourth,
the unwanted daughter—my mother,

                        was born. When did her palms

turn to steel? Child given extra
work, less education than her sisters, even less play?

These hands so old now, so brave,

what did they dream? These hands that taught us how

to light our Shabbat lamps? When did they have soft
                    skin? How wise these hands
                    webbed

with cracks, and curling early
to fit inside my father's palms. Now arms weak,

                heads bowed, they both stand by the door,

reach to touch the mezuzah,
say Shema, kiss
each other on the lips. Holding

hands when they leave
the house, she leads him—

the half-blind head of the house,
                    and takes one shaky step at a time.

Threshold

If I had walked out that night,
bag in hand, eloped,
my father couldn't have stopped me.

He wouldn't have known how,
but I knew somehow it would become
my mother's fault. Where will you go,

her eyes said. Where? I knew.
To his two-roomed flat shared by four other men
whose parents were arranging

their marriages? Or with my friend
who was not allowed to work
and was engaged to a rich boy

from her community? And I?
A runaway girl with no money
and no roof over her head

in a country where women
who left home for love ended up dead
or walked the streets. He had

told me—*Wait*. I'm getting a better job.
If it's unbearable, come. *Wait*. I knew
he was right. But what rooted

me to the floor then? Good
sense? Fear of the fate
of a disobedient daughter,

dowry-less vagabond in a predator's world?
Some great-grand aunt from granny's
photo album must've clicked

her tongue, stopped me
from leaving like this—
rebel and bride without blessing.

Taking *their* suitcase, clothes
paid for by *them*, few pieces of jewelry.
And what was really mine? A handful of rupees

and a mind packed tight with rage.
I like to say it was my practical nature
that turned me back, but I know

it was my mother's face, the way
it folded, the way she looked away,
how our present, past, and future seemed to spin

between us, how the ravine grew
into a canyon, and her silence spoke
louder than the voice of my father.

What Burns

*—for Jyoti Singh, who was raped on a bus in Delhi
   and died of fatal injuries*

Only "20% of girls are good"
hood them and tame them, or it's you they'll burn

What do you want? To be God, man, or beast?
your karma, goddesses, your crosses burn

You say smother them small! In wombs or home
no food, books, dowry, and no bra to burn

Will mercy rain on the holy who pray
who say none but devils and rebels burn

Who will remember, as we turn to ash
poet, words are witness! Make darkness burn

Nature of the Beast

There are no two ways about it.
You will get bitten.

Sometimes it's fate,

sometimes it's fatal. Whether
it's a garter or fox snake you prefer

to play with, or more sophisticated sorts—
vipers, mambas, pythons colored

like tropical forests, diamondbacks
from deserts, Amazonian

anacondas thicker
than your lover's thighs,

they're legion,

though not all lethal.
The degree of deadliness differs.

But it's just a matter of time. There are snakes
in the safest of places,
and you will get bitten.

That is the nature of the beast.

You Rise from Blue Lotuses

                              my two wooden lions—

rearing up to guard my door. Dragon-like,
your eyes
miniature head lamps

devouring darkness. What forces from without

do you drive nightly
from my trembling threshold?
Rakshasas who brawl

in backstreets and demons
in human form
will fear the ancient spells that have been sung

into your scarlet hide. Mantras
shimmer in gold dust paint. In your rough
swathe of mane lie hidden

a hundred eyes that read the thoughts of the living and the dead.

Stand strong
upon these fragile blue petals,
let the carved lotus at your feet

anchor deep,
grow roots through cement. Be David's star,
deflect Mephistopheles,

keep Beelzebub at bay. We are only
as strong as the weakest one, my brave lions—
and I am faint of heart. Sleep

not for a moment, keepers of our gate!
I have seen
how green shine the eyes

in smiling faces, how rabid

their thoughts. With the mighty arc
of your leaping bodies shield us,
we who dwell within thin walls.

Life of a Goddess

I. The Making of Durga

What are goddesses made of?

Hooghly silt
shells and sweat
milk and silk and blood
iron and bones and holy ashes
flesh and fire

II. What the Hands?

The maker's hands are hardened by fire
yet pliant like wax
as they mold

the petals that are her lips
the red river of vermillion

rushing in the ravine
that parts her kohl black hair

III. The Body Rising

Watch the ten arms grow
out of her slender trunk

fingers of electricity
hold drums conches weapons

her neck garlanded with multifoliate
lotuses radiant immortal

IV. Her Eyes

Three eyes has she
boats ablaze
in the ocean of her face

brightest is the eye inside
the eye in her forehead

torching a tunnel
from this world
to the next

V. Her Heart

We know not what breathes there but know only this

the hands that shaped its four chambers then
shape them now
that it hides beneath
the necklace of enemy heads

that on the first dawn of Dussehra

> dhak-beaten
> mantra-driven
> it quickens into flame

VI. She Rides

ten earthly days she rides on a lion

> who with gaping mouth and bloody fangs
> shreds the flesh
> of the buffalo demon

the roar resounds

Durga drives her trident
into the heart of evil

Mahisasur is dead

the drums break night's doors

VII. On the Last Day the Worshippers

the women who fell at all her feet
like rain to parched ground
                              now gather for her leaving

they shower
hibiscus and marigolds wet with dew
wipe her face with cool paan leaves

                    O mother of a hundred daughters
                    when will you return

fragrant they have bathed at daybreak
wet hair clings to their backs
new Tangail saris damp
fragile as smoke

tongues ululate like gulls in the wind

                    the muddy river calls
                    the men release her to the waves

how the storm of conch calls shake the trees
silk-heavy and garlanded she swirls faceup to the sky

trailing clouds of saffron flowers
and prayers

                    as the Hooghly flows from their eyes

Wildcat Love

Let me brand memories of sun
  burning like the stripes of Bengal

tigers into your arching back,
  claw red rivers into skin,

tear the lobes of your ears with my teeth,
  lick your wounds and your ragged places,

lap your wet lips,
  and taste our bittersweetness.

We gather our mingled essence,
  like harvest,

rest in it. At sunrise, searching
  the empty space beside you,

you cup the blood of the morning
  sun flowing through the window.

The room stirs with the echo
  of moans. You remember heat,

a rasp of tongues, my last bite,
  the lingering scent of me.

Catch

It's the fish
                     she fries in oil, and the chilies
                                  stinging the air with acrid tales,

scenes of your native
                     dark-skinned fisherwoman, sarong
                                  clinging, black tresses plastered,

sweat and sea glistening
                     on sunbaked skin
                                  that lures you. It's the turning,

the timing. Spring rush
                     thumping in rivers and veins,
                                  a sudden heat. And the story

you tell is about a pale winter memory
                     you dust off the fins
                                  of last year's trophy. Nuanced

is the wine you bring her that night; her fish eyes ask
                     Have a drink?

How easily
                     you're hooked. Her loneliness

the naked fish
                     sizzling in the pan.

Lady Lotus Eater

To escape—

and tired of the taste of our humble bread,
we left—

wanting so much more;

we chose strange paths and dreamed
new dreams. Together we toiled

the ever-climbing waves,
reaching this land where it is seemed

always afternoon. But we flounder now,
we two, the ennui seeping in every day,

the strange languages wearisome—
when we speak, that is. We never

ask each other where we are headed
or if we will ever leave

this lotus-filled land; stopped
wondering why we cannot remember

how to read the stars,
but we stand each alone

on the quays of different oceans.
Ah, but a woman's lot is not

much different here—
it is only *I* who will drown. My boat

is not seaworthy now, no match
for Scylla and Charybdis. It cannot

plough the watery main alone.
                    Why then, should I

not rest? Reap the pleasures

of our long labor, sacrifice,
good fortune? I shall ride

this island like a queen,

watch the men harvest,
savor this fine fruit,

drink this languor;
                    and my heart is safe—

locked

in a teak chest
buried in the sands

of a country I can barely recall;

inside I stored old maps,
and letters he once wrote me
in a language we knew

when we were young
and in love.

Glass Bangle Song

Hear them sing
her grandmother said to her mother
she said remember

take these circles of glass for your tiny wrists, my little one
they will clink-clink around your soft hands at the stove
when you feel the heat hit your face, they will clink
as they work, heat of boiling milk spilling over
heat on glass and flesh and on this thin gold one
your father gave me, the one his mother never got her hands on
the one I saved for you, only you

her mother said
here are some bangles, child with a lucky mole on your chin
I know he will one day buy you
so many (she smiled) bangles and he will, look how pretty
the colors, like Holi
like queen Holika burning in spring bonfires at night
and the raucous drums and tambourine shuddering all night
cool spring night

take care of him she said
you are nothing

without

him

like the air between empty fingers
the space within
radiant
see the circles, the sweet tinkling
clinking ice-like

glass song
born of fire and spun candy

said remember
do not let him hear
the sounds of your tongue, sharp as broken shards
he will cut it out
do not let your bangles talk too much
when he sleeps, glass or conch
shell wrapped around your wrist
like twisted silk
let him hear you always, working working
how your bangles chink-chink when you work
never silence them, these rings of light

for they will blame
you for his death
they will break

your bangles should he die, crush
the bones of your little hands
(she held my hands)
O feed him
well, even if you go hungry

let him listen to the music
of these rows and rows
of rainbow-filled rings,
play them like a sarangi whose magic
song wins his heart
away from his mother (she
showed me
her bare wrists)

your bangles
let them sing louder and louder if you are sad
child, listen to your widowed mother
(she wiped her eyes)

he is life

and his death
will break each shiny circle
they will circle you till they break

break your beating glass heart
your song
you

Black-Eyed Susan

Back she breaks
through swamp and mud,
and her black eyes smile

holding secrets

as deep as the sky.
Like all her once bright-faced sisters

now crushed by boot heels,

she will bloom again
in her season. Curls spilling, her bruised body

leans into the sun, and weeps petals

to the wind,
fights quietly the thunder

in the air, the scythes in the fields,
bends to shield her children,

shows them what strong roots they have.

Bus Window in the Sun

Your face in the window. Falling to pieces.
The window saw your face. Uneven, fragments,
chipped bits, a pattern

aslant, hieroglyphics.
Saw your lip synced words.
Words brought to their knees,

a bitter bubble of air,
glitter of teeth. The engine kicked in
as it always did. A roar.

Smell of diesel,
burned dust and vomit. I braced
myself for it—the jerk forward

and back, plucked
harp string come unstrung.
No song you sang could turn me back.

The jerk forward and back,
and beneath me, the seat worn
in patches like an old song,

rough and smooth and drowsy.
I settled, I settled into the hard seat,
settled into the rocking

of the bus. Bird on a swaying wire
in a storm blown past. My blanket
a sweet bandage. Fallen book

dog-eared at my feet. My eyes shot
by afternoon sun. Then your hollow
words scratching the window. Blue

notes. Hieroglyphics.
Glass. Shards. The window
watching your face.

The face watching.
The window watching the faces
fall to pieces.

Weep, Willow, Weep,

weep it all out of you, then! Your body
is bent low. They have taught you well—accept
that slap of wind, this angry blast of rain,
scourge, storm, whims of gods and unknown forces,
the crucifix's weight. Is this your fate?
Your nail-like leaves hang in rows of crosses,
your heart, wrought from stars and earth, bears seven
scars. And what was your sin? To be alive?
Spring, not sorrow, is eternal, graceful
one. You have bled life away in prayerful
weeping. Enough! Now let your hair fly loose,
you wild woman you. Madonna of trees,
rise from your bleeding knees, lift up your head,
tear the bare heavens open with your teeth!

The Kitchen Table

My grainy tongue
tastes blood when she slices
her finger while chopping

vegetables, her cry sharp,
piercing the startled air. When
she cradles her head,

on me, her hair spills
thoughts. I have watched
her fingers stroke the knife's edge

in the folds of her yellow apron.
When he's home, she dresses me
in green paisley, her damp

temples drip. She feeds
her children, sweetly, slowly,
and lets them ride my back,

play hide and seek about my legs—
only when he's gone. Her broken wings
have healed now, and her fingers

when they scrub me after dinner
signal she will be ready
soon. When she has drawn

the faded curtains against
the moon, he'll stumble in,
slump his reeking

weight on me. She will move
swiftly in the dark, and I will arch
my spine, my oaken bones

to hold him fast
till I taste his blood
on the altar of my tongue.

The Albatross's Call

Sailor, you shot me from the bluest sky,
      spun me like a scarf,
            danced under wind-filled sails.

My wings shuddered shut as you
      sang of good fortune to come.
            You thought my blood-specked

beak fallen open and useless
      could call up no storms?
            This body is real. I'm the alabaster

bird you chose with your cross-
      bow. Your very own charm
            to hang about your neck till

we turn into a heap of hard-bleached bones
      on the undone decks of a ship
            never reaching harbor or home.

Siege

Cut the engine   the guide shouts
        there must be more than fifty
the orcas' dorsal fins   slice arcs
        like swords white saddled backs   break surface
                                                we are

      surrounded

deep swoosh of sound
        suck and hiss of steam
sunless morning heaped with cumuli
        erupts with spray   they hover   beneath the skin

get closer   my face wet   five more to starboard
        I lean over   two to port   steady now
explosions of air   mirrored ocean
        long smoke trails   in silver fields   Leviathan breath
                                                tribes meet

Pacific pods gather in summer
        mushroom clouds blow   glassy roofs of water
ring of males   sea warriors we hear   the moans
        on the hydrophone   booming   chest and heart
                                                and muscle

now three now six   bulbous islands swell
        like bellies   shiny   black   slick
then plunge   pull downward immense   hollows

dark wake   just like   swirls   in my slow dream
                                                of whales

but slower   and more silvery   brush of hot breath
        on my chill skin   our boat now ambushed

an hour   can they ever forgive
        the slaughter   do they remember kin   and the unweaned
                                                        the calves

we have stolen   wail

for their mothers   smash foreheads
against glass   walls of blue pools
        hear our children cheer   O how merciful
                                          are the great

voices vibrate up through   my palms
        they fade now   my words   are rain
the big ships   wait   somewhere   in the distance

hide please hide   rising up to breathe
to die   what fifty lashing tails could do
what one whale   just one   if she wanted

Warrior Woman

Inside my bones
live an anguished people,

countries of fear,
trembling children,

and in my blood there are seas
on fire, burning boats,

broken oars. My heart, like Troy,
is a battered citadel and fears

the fine edge of your sword, your next
betrayal. Look! Your feet turn

to cloven hooves. Again how
the beauty of your wooden horse

disarms me! Then I throw
open my gates

and your blaze
devours everything. You think it's

the end. But I remember
your face. Beware.

I have already risen
from the ruins of my burning city.

Rabiya: In Mourning

I.

Are you saying namaz for my mother, Rabiya?
    Do you search for us? Where will we find you?

With your bowed and weary legs, in agony you climbed three flights
of steep stairs to our apartment when you heard your old *ma ji*, died.
How your loud wails shook the door, your unabashed weeping tore
the hallway into shreds of red. Your sobs were the throbbing ache
imprisoned in my dumb mouth.

Your unleashed
        words shouted what my riven
        heart could not.

My arms held your shaking frame. Rubi was holding her when she
breathed her last. Let me see her, you cried. Mummy's not here,
Rabiya. Kept in the box of ice. *Baraf ka buksa.* Yes, they waited for
me to arrive. Come. I'll take you to baba now. Hai Allah, you say,
what will he do without her?

Yes, we will bring her home tomorrow, say prayers, then take her
to Keoratala burning ghat. No, not burying her. She did not want
that. Say namaz for her, dear Rabiya. Let her feel no sorrow at our
separation.

She will hear you. Rock back
        and forth in holy prayer,
kneel, hold your hands
        up before your face, your closed eyes,
sing your songs, Rabiya,

I will hear you, wherever you are.

Our tears will cause a flood and she will ride in a boat
on the waves of the sea of salt
that we make together.

Rest tonight, dear Rabiya. You are frail as my mother's gray hair.
Tomorrow,
                    wrapped in a simple white sheet
and in the mist
                    of our sorrow
we will bring mummy home. At noon, we will carry her downstairs,
place her in the hearse. Load up the wreaths of cosmos and white
lotuses, bouquets of roses, gladioli, carnations, garlands of marigolds
and tuberoses, tuck them around her still body. Bring the incense
and candles neighbors give us to burn.

The traffic will stop. The policemen will bow their heads in a na-
maste to her departed soul. All passersby will do the same. The
crows and sparrows she fed with leftovers from her plate will watch
from the trees outside our window.

Walk slowly Rabiya,
to the glass doors
of the battered hearse,

whose driver is an old Sikh man dressed in white whose eyes are
quiet.

Walk slowly up to her
whom you love,
                    sing your duas.
                    Say khuda hafiz.
She will hear you.
She will thank you,
touch the top of your head, and say
don't cry.
But you will weep a river. And so will I.
And you will step back from her body which has shed its soul.

A chorus of weeping sweeps toward us. Is it Najma, Hamida, Padma, and some others I see in the crowd? The vendors and shopkeepers on Bright Street and in the Park Street area, the fruitwallahs, the bishtis, the beggars and rickshaw-pullers, line the street. I climb into the hearse. The driver starts it up, it begins to move. They move with it for a while, then a few children and two dogs begin to run by the hearse's side. I hear wails as the hearse picks up speed, glides faster into the traffic.

You are standing still
      with your white widow's pallav
            pulled over you face
                  like a shroud. It is heaving.

We are both screaming but there is no sound.

2.

Six? Seven? How old was I when you first came to work for us? My polio-wasted limbs had just learned to walk again.

How many years
did you cook and clean for us? How you perfected the rich mutton curry mummy taught you to make. How many times you were scolded, how many times you scolded us. You carried my schoolbag full of books while I labored up the stairs. How tightly you held me when I cried because I could not run with the children playing outside.

How you wailed when granny died and when we left the house with her body. And when Fatima's husband took her away from Karachi (now she's forgotten Urdu) to Kabul, when you heard she had no passport, that she would never return to Kolkata. And how you howled like a beaten animal when you heard I was leaving for America. Mummy, who had been silent till then, broke like a dam. I swallowed rising bile. How could I look her in the eyes? Or you?
          We were torn
          into pieces that day

and scattered over the desert. O Rabiya,

your keening
will rip through the wilderness
and find our lonely ears.

I was your Fatima, all over again. My playmate, Gone. Like my
mother. Like me. Gone. Again. How will we find her now? Her
husband visits sometimes, when he comes across the border with
guides who smuggle him in via secret routes. Over the mountains
and through Pakistan. Too risky to bring Fatima. She is now the
mother of clans in feudal Afghanistan. Remember when you told
me that you finally met your eldest grandson? He was a man of 17.
His first time over the mountains and through the secret passes.
Your son-in-law translated your Urdu into Pashtu so your grandson
could understand. Fatima cannot speak our languages anymore. She
cannot come, even if you are dying. Rabiya,

how will I know if you are dead? Your address is lost, our apartment
locked, our things left as if we never left on the day ma dropped

to the ground. Who will answer
                                   if you ring and ring
the dusty doorbell?
Quader, your son, will half-carry you up the stairs. Our wooden
mezuzah protects our door. For how long? How long? The thug
landlord will not even let you through the iron gate to pray on her
anniversary. You will say your prayer on the street and he will throw
your precious flowers in the gutter. You will curse the evil man, and
return.

Sway your body like a reed, Rabiya,
and say duas for us. Let me hear you
through the raging winds in my head.
The breaking branches, the deluge.
Let your words be a raft, a salvation.
                                   My heart

was a tortured bird throwing itself against the locked window when I first saw her body in the *baraf ka buksa* place. A squalid room, the owner half drunk, the attendants glassy-eyed, shabby. I stroked her cheek, her hair. Such great love and such great sorrow surged inside me all at once. I thought my chest would explode.

How peaceful she is now.
She is gone where you and I cannot go. Not yet.
My heart
    is a stone
    inside my empty husk.
    My echoing chest
    a well of bones.
    Your wails rend me now.
    Shatter, shatter
    this heavy stone
        of desolation.
        Your words are her epitaph.
Humko aadmi banaya, you cried. She made me human, made a true human being of me, you repeated like a surah that day. Your praise rides on the ether that carries her soul.

Lash the sky with your mourning,
        shout over the gale
        the ninety-nine names of Allah,

call out our names. We drift in this fog of lostness. I will come back to *Bakriwallah galli*, knock on every door, ask for you. We will search for Fatima, for my mother.
        Rabiya, listen, do you know,
        before we gave her to the fire,
as I bent to say good-bye—

a smile hovered on her lips?
I see your broken-toothed mouth
moving as if speaking from afar.

                      I lie down
                      next to my sleeping mother.
                      She snores softly. I put my arm
                      around her. I feel her breath. She stirs.

              But Rabiya, where did she go?

Pray to the One *in whose hands*
is the realm of all things
and to whom we will all
return. Your voice
                  will pierce through
                      this never-ending night,
                      this unforgiving emptiness.

Such Shifting

it took at first to balance my body in air,

tilting this way and that, finally
rising. Soon I cast away

my beginnings, its branches
howling at the soles of my feet,

and as if air was all that mattered
and all that I wanted to be—

I denied my shadow,
watched it flake like dead
skin. But earth's tectonic

bones will drag back
its own. To life.
Or burial. A winged seed

lifts off, madly in love

with the wind. A world
made of elsewhere

lives in its veins. Restless

different element.
Reckless. We try flight,

learn to fall.

Strange Landing

The air smells different here,

the airport looks dressed up, people cold.
I dread the immigration officer. Eyes

check my passport, my face. He asks
so many questions. My dullness

annoys him. One more scouring look from him,
and I'm through. Everything hurts.

On the other side, the carousel groans.

I look for my suitcases—bought secondhand
in a battered street where an aunt took me—
bargained with the shop owner in a way
only she could, her oily voice beating him down,
then me peeling precious rupees from my wallet.

Suddenly I am glad to be far from all that.
My lumpy luggage appears—
islands carrying the ragged spirit

of home, my history, my geography.
My future, my past wrapped
in the skin of the present—

the bleeding torn skin of the now.

My trapped woman-heart pounds,
my girl-child feet freeze. How do I
force myself out into the thick air

surging behind those glass doors?

I find a porter, learn they are called skycaps.
He is handsome and I feel shy. His giant
hands lift my suitcases as if they were tissue.
He sweeps me toward Customs. I trot
behind him, flustered. My mouth

utters soundless apologies like mantras
to the skycap, the officer, the airport,
my hurtling suitcases, my Bob Dylan cassettes
and the bottle of Bengal mustard
squeezed last minute into my handbag,

to my hands, to my face, to the air I breathe,

and most of all to my husband
whose face I suddenly can't remember.

God Bless You

they say when you sneeze,
lest your soul be stolen by the devil.

Maybe the man with the close-set eyes
and silver crucifix who followed me

into bus number 36 at Devon and Broadway
knew this, as he God Blessed me a few times and
browbeat me with the word of the Lord.

The bus whined as its ill-balanced body
swayed like a howdah on the back of an elephant.
Turning up his voice, he said,
You are Hindu, and pray to Shiva,
maybe Moslem . . . pray to Allah

and I moved a seat closer to the bus driver,
who looked away. I lost hope of ever being saved.
But after addressing several speeches to my back,

he faced me before getting off and said, *I will pray*
the devil won't get your soul, God bless you.

And then one day, sprawled in the grass
off Lake Shore Drive in August sunshine,
I watched the Blue Angels

streak the sky,
white trails vanish over quivering water,
everyone clapped and said
God bless America, and I saw the pilot

in the bubble of the cockpit wave
as my ears exploded with sound—

crashing like a waterfall inside me.

How it flies from the tongue—

God bless you, like "He" was really there,
all ears, all heart, all everything,
with nothing to do

but bless, bless, bless.
And I really wondered who was blessing who
and for what, and if we were all as blessed
as the Nike-sneakered, white-robed,
black-bearded Jesus I saw at the Blues

Fest in Grant Park, who pulled
a huge wooden cross on wheels

and who only smiled as he handed out papers,
eyes glinting *God bless yous* through long hair
flowing through his crown of thorns.

Hibiscus and Smoking Incense

are wedged near a plastic picture
of red-tongued goddess Kali

on the dashboard
of the blue Nissan minibus. Her slanted

eyes large, her third eye

hypnotic.

A Hindi film song
plays on tape. A woman's husky voice
moans, Oh oh what's beneath my blouse?

Choli ke peeche kya hai
Choli ke peeche kya hai

Oh it's my heart, oh my heart, she sighs,
it beats, it beats beneath my blouse. Shyamal

our jagged-toothed
driver revs the engine.

Hollers

at honking cars centimeters away.
A garland of milk-white jasmine hangs

below the rearview mirror,
swinging madly. The sweet smell

is stifling. I close my eyes. Into

the roaring river of morning traffic,
the boat

is launched, small metal
bubble with its thin blue skin

How Often on Himalayan Roads

—*after Agha Shahid Ali*

have I seen warnings:
it is better to be late, Mr. Driver
than to be the late Mr. Driver

and wondered who really heeded
these slogans painted on rocks
near the most dangerous

curves in the mountains,
because the truck and bus drivers,
reckless as gods, never did. It was I,

frightened bird from the delta
of the Hooghly who quaked
seeing the sheer drop, the landslides

that could stop up my path,
and how I could become the captive
elephant who was forced off the cliff

by Huns who wanted to hear it scream
and whose mother still searches,
searches. You wrote about your falling

even as you fell. These mountains
birthed you. Your footprints
are everywhere! The trail

is here. My feet are small, unsteady.
How could I have known my way
then? The road would disappear

and I would lose and find again
that veiled path,
a distant dream of my country.

Chimes

I hear uneven silver sounds,
chimes—

outside the window
of our first apartment in America,
on West Aldine, Chicago, and the tinkling

like the chatter of children,
voices that woke me in the mornings
on days I didn't want to wake,

or mornings I didn't know
if I was still in Kolkata, hearing
the night clatter of the Bright Street restaurant—

its skinny child servers
scrubbing soot-black dekchis
and pots twice as large
as them. Lids clang, spoons fall,

the owner shouts. Harsh night music that rips
through the chorus of barking
street dogs. Still I hear

every word of their lewd stories, loud laughter,
learn words that sting my mouth
like acid, their vileness strangely
satisfying. High voices

cracking, they sing Hindi film songs
under the street lamp, tease
the drunk, the homeless, the mad,
then fight each other till blood

stains the pavement. Midnight
son et lumière of the street
when I tossed on damp sheets, and sleep
would not come. Rough play over,

they wash clothes, bathe their weary
boy-man bodies, climb to the windowless
attic to sleep. How long?

How long? Soon the thin
percussion of tin spoon
and plate. Skinny hands

chopping, pounding,
rolling dough. Beggars gather
at first light, bodies hunched
against the blue wall with graffiti

in Bengali and Urdu,
ask for food. The first customers
call for chai-bishkoot. Bathers
at the hand pump curse louder than the cawing

of crows. Children wait at the corner
for school buses. The smell of fried puris,
the heat from steaming alu bhaji
wafts up to me. I am getting dressed

for school, can't find clean socks,
my mother is calling,
but strange—it is still dark,

a *Chicago Tribune* truck pulls up,

the delivery man's boots
crunch fresh snow. On Lake Shore Drive
The 145 moans, children
shout to each other on their way
to Nettelhorst Elementary. Asleep

beside me, you stir, your arms jerk,
your alarm's slow beep
not reaching you. I wake you gently.
You are late for work. Maybe, you too

saw again your street,
heard your mother's call,
heard the school bell ring as you dashed
through closing gates, and maybe,

you too heard the chimes—
the ones I heard last night,

tin scraping on tin,
captive voices singing.

City of Hibiscus Eyes

The song I lost is looking for me
but I don't know how to reach it
it wanders where the red hibiscus grows
I remember sounds like falling petals

I don't know how to reach
those fading words, the shadowy eyes
all I remember is petals, like falling phrases
they slip away just as I catch their scent

the hibiscus songs, the purple whispers
memories of dust, Kolkata summers
they slip away as I catch their scent
so soft, so hooded with silence

memories of dusty Kolkata summers
my seeking fingers, your searching eyes
so dark, so hooded in silence
like flowers I gathered you in my arms

your searching eyes, my seeking fingers
fill the void with words unsaid
I gather you in my arms like flowers
my lost song hovers, I hear it sigh

the city watches with hibiscus eyes
as I gather you in my arms like flowers
but then you fall away in the smoky dusk
the song I lost keeps looking for me

Child of Churning Water

My salty songs
sound no different

than the gull's. My shadow hovers—
I see my mouth opening
and closing in air,

as if calling. No words
but breath escapes my throat,
I hear the murmur

of ocean. Who shall I be now?
Where can I perch?

My woman heart is bird of the sea and fish of the air,
blood and dirt,

leaf and light, child

of churning
water. My feet
are whales; I shall

dive deep,

turn to kelp
and pearl. Tides speak
history and planets

read my palm.
My breath is
writ in water.

See, now I am leaf boat
on the river Ganga,

my clay-lamp soul
drifting on mist-hidden seas

to shores only stars can know.

Death of a Frog

—Philautus maia, first and only specimen ever to be found,
circa 1860, in Sri Lanka

Maya: Illusion

And who were your ancestors,
your glossy little children, lone
ghost of the emerald

swamp? Was your landscape
just a projection of some *heat-oppressed*
brain? Dead, you tell us

you existed. A museum's
your mausoleum now. It seems
Maia slept as you were taken,

and the furrow in the field
did not swallow you like it did Sita. But
here you are—a brown bauble

captive under glass. Habeas
corpus. Plucked from
a rain-heavy lotus leaf

(or was it from an algae-slathered
river?) by the hands
of your discoverer. Left your webbed

footprint in the mud we claim
as ours. And, making up
stories as we go, we gather

our basketfuls of Eves
and Adams, fallen
Lucifers, snakes and whales;

but you
fell somewhere by the side
of that old road. The sun

touched you once
in that forest. You glowed,
then you were gone.

Maya: Compassion

Hard to tell what color your eyes
were. Your skin tone under the true sun?
Shriveled water-loving

land-living issue of mudskippers,
carcass of lost knowledge, O maya!
This ache—is it just illusion?

Weep for the passing of birds
and beasts! Even St. Francis
intervened for you. See, he wipes

his eyes with his sleeve. And after,
did St. Peter welcome you? Or like
our colonist fathers measured,

filed you away? You were the last
of your line. Rest now. My fingers
anoint you with moisture. My prayers

ravel around you in ether. Not yet
ashes, not yet dust,
we preserve you. In this life,

we resurrect you. Through
your descendants still unborn,
still unrisen from the wet lands.

Holy amphibian,
child of earth and water,
when will you come again?

Borer

I inherit hard jaws and hunger
from the genes of my ancestors—

to delve deep into bark, pith, bole,
oblivious to all but my desire

for light at the end

of the tunnel. I eat
through ringed history,

seven years of famine, seven of plenty,
taste the movement of seas,

the ice invasion, plague, fire,
pestilence and flood,

and can even hear
hoofbeats of horsemen. And I

hard-bodied, long-legged beauty
with beaded antennae

am destined to devour,
drive my stake

through hearts of trees,
my nail through the palm

of every hand that feeds me.

Dark-Bitter-Sweet

Mother see I make an altar for you
a table covered with dark chocolate you craved

Dove, Hershey's, Ghirardelli chocolates I carried for you
over the continents and seas
how you would savor them piece by piece
after lunch and after dinner and quietly when no one was looking
and in between times
suck on them while you lay in bed sleepless
reading *The Telegraph* and *The Times*
reading yellowed books that piled up
with the medicines on the small bedside table
reading the same *Reader's Digests* over and over
till you feel asleep at one or two a.m.

for those lonely midnight snacks
you kept little chocolate hearts and kisses and squares
in little Ziplocs by your pillow
chocolates half-melted with a few hopeful ants wandering
O this chocolate from far far away by your bedside mother
at least it thrilled your tongue for a moment

this time when I visited I saw how ashen your face was
how deep the circles under your eyes
you told me you had stopped brushing your teeth
I have only a few anyway you said *why should I care*
you laughed when I told you the dentist would get scared
if he looked into your mouth
the only time you laughed this visit
the only time I heard a broken chuckle like a cross
between the gurgle of a hidden scream and a cough

sweet chuckle I will hear over and over
forgive me mother, I had forgotten the sound of your laughter
I had forgotten how to make you laugh

mother every good-bye was a death
so why do I cry now that you've left
you whom I abandoned time and time again
why do I rage against your leaving, rage against your not raging
Rubi, your maid and companion, held you
you gasped—soft hiccup, head falling upon your chest
(O sweet body I had bathed and clothed but two weeks ago)
your shoulders slumping (O darling shoulders
that I bathed, smoothed Vaseline lotion upon
but twenty days ago) too late to save too late to say too late too late
too soon too quick too soon your breath escaped

mummy under the chiffon chunni we draped around your head
I hid a handful of dark chocolates
before the men with the cold eyes tending to the furnaces beckoned
and we lifted you, surrendered your body
to rows of fire teeth, the brick walls reflecting red
the shadow of torn roses upon your sleeping face
(your wrinkled face I washed but twenty days ago)
the iron door clanged shut like a prison

these chocolates mother may they make you forget all pain
(when I hid them I saw you smile)
forgive us mother our small selfish lives
ma I'll make an altar for you
build a dark-bitter-sweet chocolate temple for you

A Gathering

                    To drown this dying
November dusk
the crows have arrived

                    in locust numbers,
                    come to rend the leaden air

with their incessant
cawing. Calls fall thick
as arrows, rise up again in
                              unintelligible words
                              expounding great
                              woe or wisdom,

maybe tales of diaspora followed
by light evening gossip?
The aged offering
                              rules of survival?
                              More clouds
                              of verbose souls blow in,

rest, then pass. Rest,
then pass. A perpetually changing
guard, a host of shadow angels,
                              symmetry settling,
                              shattering. Such raucous opera,
such concentric swirls
of travelers, a frantic vertigo
                              before winter shuts us
down like a tomb full of worms
and dirt. Is there no hope?
                    Voices rasp high and low—
                    rusty trumpets

full of secrets.
See how they heave themselves up
                          like one brutal animal,

            then break
            into strings, and whorls,
            curls, cloud-calligraphy,

a vortex collapsing. Tonight
the fingernail moon
                          hangs on the lean beak
of the horizon. In the half light
they stir and stream, live flowing
obsidian lava pulsing in
                  one mighty river from the edge

            of another world. Doom? Death?
            O these daggers of memory,
            visiting spirits. Yes, these are
my prophets, my ancestors,
the living and the dead
come to visit, remind,
                        my history
                        arriving. See this fresh murder

settling in the oaks outside my window?—
Full of feisty young-bloods

sure to jive and jibe at the stars
till dawn. Old souls among them
tilt their heads
            and watch. May their ancient
            music dwell in the house

            of these branches
            and on cruelest days

fill my ears with mystery
                           words, my eyes overflow like a cup of wine

with the memory of their visit,
let me remember again
how they resurrect themselves,

               how they beat back
               the wings of silence.

Bees, Sunday Brunch

How easily you boasted (you who
rarely brag) as you poured the Amarone,
about your victory,

the beehive

that grew into a city inside the lip
of the fancy brick façade
beneath your window;

your kind face suddenly split into smiles,
into many planes (like a Picasso
painting), and pointing you explained

how the cancerous hive had grown—
and how impossible, at first,
it had been to get to its humming

heart; so sweet the moment was, you said,

when the vacuum cleaner
sucked out the hidden cells,
the golden lives, the royal jelly,

the sudden burst of energy that filled you,

when your finger pressed the power button
(like God's finger touching Adam's
in the blue of the Sistine sky). It was good,

you said, to watch the broken beads
in the stream of honey and crushed
wax pulsing through the translucent pipe.

And then when it was done, the twisted rope
of furry shapes you flung like a dead
serpent into the thicket beyond your tidy lawn—

the strange chain of lifeless bodies
and debris of vanquished city
breaking in air as it fell,—

was it heavier than you thought?

Garuda, King of Birds

*—inspired by an 18th-century painting based
on a story from the Ramayana*

I.

His immense eagle-human form
flies across a sky so pale it must be dawn,

and the sea far beneath
his upswept white-feathered wings

is silvery and calm. Below stretches a thin green line
of shore, of plants and flowers painted in fine detail—

purple iris, scarlet poppy. On a diagonal that fills blue space,
in garments as gold as his jewelry,

his pearl-sheened image rises, skin milk-white,
swordlike bronze talons. In the parting

of curved wings, sit Krishna and Radha,
heads held together in a gilted halo,

wearing red, necks draped with jewels.
Wielding the lotus, conch, chakra, and mace,

the blue god of cowherds—avatar of Vishnu,
chose him, lord of birds, to ride.

Krishna is his king, but on this canvas
Garuda is the sun.

2.

Garuda only stole the moon to save his mother,
hid its silver face under his wing.

Devourer of evil, and a god himself,
he outflew the armies who pursued him,

defeated all with slashing talons, havoc-
wreaking beak. He won, but his big heart relented,

returned with grace the captive moon. His
reward? That he become the eternal

vehicle of Vishnu, protector of the good,
stay loyal to the Preserver

of the Universe and his every avatar. And then
in Ayodhya, he appeared as Jatayu,

battled Ravana in the skies, tore at his ten heads
with his claws as he carried

captive Sita in his flying chariot. Maybe
the heavens were as pale as this one in the painting,

when the demon hacked his wings. Garuda
plummeted, the sky raining blood and feathers.

Rama rushed there, but could only cradle the crownless head,
shut the lids of those once-fierce eyes with his fingers.

The Magi

The three wise women
rode silently on their donkeys,
saddlebags full of gifts,

water and food for the road. The sky
shone over the hut as they dismounted
by the door. They heard

drinking songs from the inn, the clatter
of wine jugs. Robes trailing
in dirt, they carried the bundles

in their strong arms, and looking inside
they saw the child that lay
in the thin woman's lap. The brown

eyes of doves, restless
on the crossbeam looked
down at the women,

their words whistling briefly on the night
wind as it stirred for a moment
the feathers that covered

their tiny hearts. Even the skittish
goats, the rooster and his hens
were silent. The women left

blankets, herbs, salve, honey. Then
wept as they propped a heavy
bolt of white cloth against

the wall—for no curse they'd flung,
or stone, diverted the horse
that had followed them, its hooves

churning up the hard winter
ground when it passed,
its pale hide shimmering,

and victory reflected in the ice
of its eyes, as it charged on
in the light of the already dying star.

As Birds Do

—*from Macbeth*

I feed them here, on my deck, ma;
they know how to find food—the last flock
of migrants flitted pale yellow,

too quick for me to look.
My thoughts dart
to the nuthatch approaching

my feet. With this scattering of seed
I coax them—settle please,
here, here. I have forgotten

their ways, ma, how to tilt my raptor body
through the woods, burgundy eyes
on target. Or was I a weaver

of leaf cradles—rocking high
at the mercy of the wind; or a downy
pecking out a home

in bark? And could these bony feet
have danced in marshes with the cranes?
My wing-beats slicing through November

cold for thousands of miles as I called
out to you? How will I know my way?
Are we both hummingbirds,

ma, who crave summer's reprieve?
Can our whirring hearts hold steady
when we fear the fickle winds?

Somewhere Deep

in oceans of coral, of kelp,

lie cliffs and caves unknown,
where soundless creatures of the dark—

immensely old and primal live
as if Time did not exist

and shadows move like mountains.
I listen to the violins of murky hearts—

coelacanth and crustacean,
thunder of manta wings,

whispers of shellfish in sand.
So well I know your boat

that travels my skin, makes love to my storms,
you, who dive deep to feel my pulse,

explore my salt and water world,
the weight of waves

crushing your bones. We reach
and touch, my arms hold you close,

I drown you in love, feed your dreams
to the fish of my flesh, the hungry abyss

of my soul. Your breath rises
like the bubble nets of humpbacks,

and I am sadder than their songs, my sorrow
howling long and low through the night

like a whale calling her lost calf.

Listen

to the waves
to the voices of children calling from the sea

for the ears of the deaf shall bear the weight of water
not a fish glinting blue, not a green turtle amid dead coral cities

make peace then

with the sky and those who live in its arms
with the sparrows who build nests in your rafters

O heavy
are the curses that will rain upon your head
brown feathers drift in the silence, your roof is chaff

shelter with your hands

the spider that crawls
across the palm of your page, free her in the grass

atone
O stonehearted one, listen

beware
the unsleeping
    eyes of inconsolable goddesses

            neither candles nor incense
            will appease

            will staunch the flood

                    of their weeping

ACKNOWLEDGMENTS

My deepest gratitude to John for his support, patience, compassion, and love. To Lorna Goodison and M. L. Liebler for their encouragement and kindness. And a special thank you to everyone at Wayne State University Press who helped to make this book happen!

Grateful acknowledgement is made to the editors of the following journals and anthologies in which these poems, sometimes in earlier versions, first appeared:

Bear River Review: "Hibiscus and Smoking Incense"

The Café Review: "How Often on Himalayan Roads." Issue on Agha Shahid Ali.

Cellar Roots: "Catch." "Incendiary" issue.

Cutthroat: "Consider the Sari." Finalist in the Joy Harjo Poetry Contest. Reprinted in *Uncommon Core: Anthology for Living and Learning*.

Driftwood: "Such Shifting" and "Dharamsala." "Such Shifting" was reprinted in *A Bird in the Hand: Risk and Flight*, an anthology.

Dunes Review: "The Blessed"; "Fire: For Beginners"; "Bees, Sunday Brunch"

HazMat: "Apples and Oranges"

Inventing the Invisible (online): "Somewhere Deep." Honorable mention in their contest and recorded for "Art in the Air" Radio show.

The Kenyon Review Online: "Death of a Frog"; "You, Without Shoes"

The MacGuffin: "The Hands that Lit the Shabbat Lamps"; "*As Birds Do*"

pacific REVIEW: "Kingdom of Sharks." Vivarium issue.

The Paterson Literary Review: "God Bless You." Editor's Choice Prize.

Peninsula Poets: "City of Hibiscus Eyes"

Solstice: "Something Falls"

"God Bless You," "Strange Landing," and "Chimes" appeared in *Lands I Live In*, a chapbook published by Mayapple Press and nominated for a PEN America Beyond Borders Award.

"The Eye of the Poppy" and "Weep, Willow, Weep," were published in *My Vision, Your Voice: An Artistic Duet*, 2012, a collaborative project involving photography and poetry, and published by the Macomb Oakland Recreational Center.

"Seeking the Snake," "Borer," "Prey," "The Albatross's Call," " Nature of the Beast," "The Kitchen Table," "Wildcat Love," "Black-Eyed Susan," "Penelope Speaks to the Women," "Somewhere Deep," and "Warrior Woman" also appeared in *What Dread*, a chapbook published by Finishing Line Press. It was a semifinalist in the New Women's Voices Contest, and was nominated for a Pushcart Prize.

"Mudras: Language of Hands" was written for an interdisciplinary collaboration called "India: A Light Within." Photographer Charlee Brodsky (Carnegie Mellon University) and Odissi dancer Sreyashi Dey were my collaborators.

"Dark-Bitter-Sweet" was selected by a jury to part of an exhibit at the Asian American Women Artists Association (AAWAA) in San Francisco.

"Penelope Speaks to the Women" won the second prize in the Springfed Arts Contest; Marie Howe was the judge. "The Blessed" won first prize; Dorianne Laux was the judge.

"Havan" won a Hopwood award at the University of Michigan.

Notes

"The Blessed"

The quote "do we not bleed, do we not die" is from Shylock's speech to Antonio, in Shakespeare's *The Merchant of Venice.*

"The Eye of the Poppy"

Lines quoted from Psalm 23; from Tennyson's poem "Break, Break, Break"; "Who Killed Cock Robin?," a folk song, the first version of which appeared in "Tom Thumb's Pretty Song Book," 1744; and "You Are My Sunshine," a popular song recorded by Jimmie Davis and Charles Mitchell in 1939.

"Turntable"

"Money Can't Buy Me Love," "It's Been A Hard Day's Night," and "I Saw Her Standing There" are popular songs by the Beatles.

"What Burns"

Some lines in the poem are extracted or adapted from newspapers and on-line reports that quoted Jyoti Singh's parents, her rapists, her rapists' lawyers.

The word "jyoti" means light.

"Lead me from darkness to light.
Lead me from death to immortality".
—Brihadaranyaka Upanishad—I.iii.28

"Lady Lotus Eater"

References Tennyson's "The Lotus Eaters" and several lines from the poem are quoted here.

"Rabiya: In Mourning"

"In whose hand is the realm of all things" is a quote from Surah Yaseen, Chapter 36:83, the Holy Qur'an. (Sahih International Translation, quran.com)

"Hibiscus and Smoking Incense"

"Choli Ke Peeche Kya Hai" is a hit song from the Hindi action thriller *Khal Nayak* produced and directed by Subhash Ghai in 1993.

"Child of Churning Water"

The phrase "writ in water" originates from a version of Beaumont and Fletcher's play Philaster, 1611: "All your better deeds shall be in water writ, but this in Marble."

But the line is better known as it appears in Keats's *Poetic Works*, 1821 and as part of the epitaph on his tombstone: "Here lies one whose name was writ in water."

"Death of a Frog"

"Heat-oppressed brain" is taken from Macbeth's speech where he sees a vision of a dagger leading him toward the chamber in which King Duncan sleeps.

"*As Birds Do*"

In Shakespeare's *Macbeth,* after Macduff's murder, Lady Macduff and her young son are talking, and she says to him, "How will we live?" and the child replies, "As birds do, mother."

"Listen"

"Thank God the scorpion picked on me / and spared my children" are the last lines of Nissim Ezekiel's poem *Night of The Scorpion,* from his collection titled *The Exact Name* published in 1965.